C000025144

WEDNESBURY
MEMORIES

IAN M. BOTT

SUTTON PUBLISHING

Sutton Publishing Limited
Phoenix Mill · Thrupp · Stroud
Gloucestershire · GL5 2BU

First published 2004

Title page photograph: Community bonfire erected in 1935 at the junction of Old Park Road and Manor House Road, in the shadow of St Mary's church, for the Silver Jubilee celebrations of King George V and Queen Mary. *(Jack Cooksey)*

British Library Cataloguing in Publication Data
A catalogue record for this book is available from the British Library.

ISBN 0-7509-3660-6

Typeset in 10.5/13.5 Photina.
Typesetting and origination by
Sutton Publishing Limited.
Printed and bound in England by
J.H. Haynes & Co. Ltd, Sparkford.

THE BLACK COUNTRY SOCIETY

The Black Country Society is proud to be associated with **Sutton Publishing** of Stroud. In 1994 the society was invited by Sutton to collaborate in what has proved to be a highly successful publishing partnership, namely the extension of the ***Britain in Old Photographs*** series into the Black Country. In this joint venture the Black Country Society has played an important role in establishing and developing a major contribution to the region's photographic archives by encouraging society members to compile books of photographs of the area or town in which they live.

The first book in the Black Country series was *Wednesbury in Old Photographs* by Ian Bott, launched by Lord Archer of Sandwell in November 1994. Since then 55 Black Country titles have been published. The total number of photographs contained in these books is in excess of 11,000, suggesting that the whole collection is probably the largest regional photographic survey of its type in any part of the country to date.

This voluntary society, affiliated to the Civic Trust, was founded in 1967 as a reaction to the trends of the late 1950s and early '60s. This was a time when the reorganisation of local government was seen as a threat to the identity of individual communities and when, in the name of progress and modernisation, the industrial heritage of the Black Country was in danger of being swept away.

The general aims of the society are to stimulate interest in the past, present and future of the Black Country, and to secure at regional and national levels an accurate understanding and portrayal of what constitutes the Black Country and, wherever possible, to encourage and facilitate the preservation of the Black Country's heritage.

The society, which now has over 2,500 members worldwide, organises a yearly programme of activities. There are six venues in the Black Country where evening meetings are held on a monthly basis from September to April. In the summer months, there are fortnightly guided evening walks in the Black Country and its green borderland, and there is also a full programme of excursions further afield by car. Details of all these activities are to be found on the society's website, **www.blackcountrysociety.co.uk**, and in *The Blackcountryman*, the quarterly magazine that is distributed to all members.

PO Box 71 · Kingswinford · West Midlands DY6 9YN

CONTENTS

Hill Top Foundry was established in 1799 at Hawkes Lane, Hill Top, West Bromwich. In 1934 these branch works were opened at the former Anchor Works in Smith Road, Wednesbury. This building was re-erected brick by brick at the Black Country Living Museum in 1984, where it now serves as the main entrance and gift shop. *(Edgar Archer)*

To the WOMEN of the
Parliamentary Borough of Wednesbury.

As I am afraid I shall not be able to call upon you all personally before next Saturday, I send you this photograph instead, but I hope that my husband's return as Member for Wednesbury will give me many opportunities of meeting you.

Yours sincerely

Madeleine V. H. Baker

VOTE FOR BAKER.

Printed and Published by ELTON & BROWN, Owen Street, Tipton.

Madeleine Baker's anticipation of her husband's return as Member of Parliament for Wednesbury ended in disappointment at the polling booths on 3 December 1910. H. Arthur Baker BA, the prospective Liberal candidate, lost out to the Conservative John Norton Griffiths, who then served the borough until 1918. Londoner Mrs Baker was the youngest daughter of Mr Joseph McGaw of Ko-a-ba, New South Wales, Australia. *(Jim Boulton)*

INTRODUCTION

The Black Country town of Wednesbury, situated in the valley of the River Tame, has origins as an Iron Age hillfort, later colonised by the Saxons who named it after Woden, their god of war. In AD 916, it was fortified by Mercian Princess Ethelfleda, daughter of King Alfred the Great, whose earthworks survive in part below the ancient parish church of St Bartholomew. William the Conqueror's Domesday Book of 1086 describes a manor consisting of ploughland and meadows surrounded with dense woodland. Much of this woodland, once part of the Royal Forest of Cannock, was later destroyed by the charcoal burners as fuel for iron smelting, until charcoal was replaced with coke (a residue of coal) in the 1750s.

Subterranean Wednesbury held vast reserves of the minerals that were to fuel the eighteenth-century Industrial Revolution, these being coal, ironstone and limestone, and fireclay used for brickmaking. Already 'cole pits' had been recorded as early as 1315 and Wednesbury Forge at Wood Green was established before 1597. Abandoned coal mines could be prone to collapse, causing 'crownings in', or spontaneous combustion, known locally as 'wildfire', both causes of widespread subsidence.

St Bartholomew's was founded in the Middle Ages, the earliest reference to a vicar being made in 1199. The Manor House stood north of the church while Oakeswell Hall lay to the south along Walsall Street. Tudor cottages lined Hancox Green, today known as High Bullen. At Wood Green the River Tame wound its way to the Delves, a farming community transferred to neighbouring Walsall and West Bromwich in boundary changes of 1930.

In 1709 Queen Anne granted the Market Charter, enabling stalls to be erected every Friday and Saturday around the Market Cross, a brick building raised on arches with adjacent stocks and whipping post, where now the clock tower stands. Here the Revd John Wesley often preached, although once infamously attacked by anti-Methodist rioters on 20 October 1743. The horseblock from which he also ministered, originally at High Bullen, is now preserved at nearby Spring Head Central Mission. One social evil in Wesley's day was the barbaric blood sport of cockfighting, immortalised in the ballad of 'Wedgbury Cocking', in which the townspeople were described as 'all savage by nature and guilty of deeds most shocking'! Unique to St Bartholomew's is the fourteenth-century gilded wooden lectern, unusual in its form of a fighting cock. Industries of this period included gun barrel forging, 'Wedgbury Ware' pottery and intricately painted South Staffordshire enamels, fired on to copper snuff boxes and the like; these are now much sought after collectors' items. Some of these fine enamels feature in HM the Queen's personal collections.

The opening of the Wednesbury Old Canal in 1769 followed by the arrival of the Walsall Canal in 1786–99 and Tame Valley Canal of 1844 linked the town's industrial sites with many rivers and ports. In 1825–6 the much-acclaimed engineer Thomas Telford improved the length of the London to Holyhead coaching route through Wednesbury, bypassing the town centre and rebuilding Wednesbury Bridge over the River Tame. The Grand Junction Railway opened at Wood Green in 1837, severing 630 acres of the rural Delves district from the town. This was followed with the South Staffordshire line in 1850 and Isambard Kingdom Brunel's Great Western Railway of 1854, now the route of the Midland Metro tramway, opened in 1998.

Establishment of the tube trade in Wednesbury during the 1820s led to the place becoming known as 'Tubetown'. In about 1851 the tubemaking district of Mesty Croft grew rapidly when the Wednesbury Building Society sold off plots of land to its shareholders, creating the distinctive community of New Town, which was further expanded with the additional council housing estate of 1928. The growth of the iron and steel trades in the nineteenth century saw the total industrialisation of the landscape with giants like F.H. Lloyd's and the Patent Shaft and Axletree Co. employing thousands, manufacturing everything metal from nuts and bolts to suspension bridges.

During the incumbency of the Revd Isaac Clarkson (St Bartholomew's, 1829–55) new ecclesiastical districts were established, these being St James in 1844, St John in 1846 and All Saints, Moxley, and St Andrew, Kings Hill, both in 1851. Following the 1832 and 1849 outbreaks of cholera the Local Board of Health was elected in 1851 firstly to tackle the town's poor sanitary conditions. This board was also to oversee the opening of Wood Green Cemetery in 1868, Municipal Offices, Holyhead Road in 1871 and Public Baths and Library, Walsall Street, in 1878.

The town's Charter of Incorporation was granted by Queen Victoria on 10 July 1886, thus creating the Municipal Borough of Wednesbury. Its first act of municipal benefaction was the opening of Brunswick Park on 21 June 1887, the Queen's Golden Jubilee day. The Art Gallery, Holyhead Road and New Theatre Royal (Hippodrome), Upper High Street, both opened in 1891. The country's first all-electric tramcar travelled from Wood Green to Walsall on 31 December 1892. The corporation electricity works opened in the Shambles in 1904.

In the summer of 1913 the town's tubeworkers went on strike for a better weekly wage. Sympathisers distributed free food, and soup kitchens were set up to feed hungry children. The following year saw the start of the First World War, during which the town suffered a Zeppelin attack on 31 January 1916, killing fourteen locals. Work began in 1919 on the Manor Farm and Wood Green housing estates. Others followed in the 1930s at Bilston Road, Dangerfield Lane, Park Lane and Friar Park West. At the same time slum clearance programmes were removing the back-to-backs built the previous century. The Second World War saw the womenfolk churning out ammunition and tanks in the town's 'shadow factories', operated under a veil of secrecy. The warship HMS *Albrighton* was adopted by the borough in 1942.

Postwar Wednesbury witnessed the integration of many ethnic groups into the community, invited to help rebuild the nation. Town-twinning links were established with the similarly industrial towns of Bourgueil in France and Kladno in Czechoslovakia. Work commenced on the Golflinks housing estate in 1949 and the Woods estate in 1960. Hydes Road playing fields, opened on 31 August 1956, were the venue for the seventy-fifth Anniversary of Incorporation celebrations, held on 8 July 1961. The Horticultural Show was held annually in Brunswick Park, and is now marked with the Town Carnival, organised by the Rotary Club each July. Her Majesty Queen Elizabeth II was warmly received on 24 May 1962 on the occasion of her visit to the borough. The M6 motorway arrived in 1966 with the construction of Junction 9 at Wood Green.

Wednesbury once returned its own Member of Parliament, including Alfred Short (MP 1918–31), Under-Secretary of State to the Labour Government, and John Stonehouse (MP 1957–71), Postmaster General, whose political career ended in disgrace in 1974 when serving as Labour MP for Walsall North. More recently Baroness Boothroyd, first Lady Speaker to the House of Commons, represented the town from 1970, firstly as Labour MP for West Bromwich, then from 1974 until retirement from politics in 2000 as MP for West Bromwich West, whose constituency includes Wednesbury.

Local government reorganisations in 1966 placed Wednesbury in the County Borough of West Bromwich, bringing to an end eighty years of self-governing status. In 1974, the whole became part of the Metropolitan Borough of Sandwell and its county status changed from that of Staffordshire to the West Midlands.

Ian M. Bott, Wednesbury, 2004

1

School Report

Each school day starts with an assembly, as seen here at Old Park Primary School, *c*. 1960. The school was built in 1952 on land bordered by Old Park Road and Woden Road North. (*Old Park Primary School*)

Class Three of St John's National School. Infants have their picture taken in 1914. The Russell Street school was built in 1848, and opened its doors on 3 November 1849. Following demolition in the late 1960s, the school's title was transferred to the nearby Board School in Lower High Street. *(Brian Broome)*

Pupils of St Mary's Convent High School are pictured alongside the shrine to Our Lady in the school gardens, 1935. The school opened in what was formerly Church Hill House in 1930 on a site now built over with 56–74 Church Hill. *(Jack Cooksey)*

Teacher Miss Gladys Steventon is seen with the pupils in her charge at St James National School, 1935. The classroom appears to be well supplied with vases of fresh cut flowers. *(Gladys Steventon)*

St James schoolchildren in a typical posed 'orchestra' photograph, 1935. The school buildings, which were erected in 1844 and extended in 1866, still stand today in the aptly named St James Street and serve as the Parish Centre. *(Gladys Steventon)*

Lower High Street Board School changed its name twice, firstly to Mountford Primary and then to St John's. Here, a Board School classroom is pictured in 1944. Pupil Diane Shepherd sits third right from the front, while fellow pupil Dorothy Benning stands third from the right at the back, identified by matching white dress and bows in her hair. The school, dating from 1880, was replaced exactly a century later with a modern building. *(Norma Caswell)*

The Red Book is the subject of a St Bartholomew's School reading class in 1957. Back row, left to right: Colin Grice, -?-, Terry Pownell, Jennifer Birks, Eunice Worthington, Janet Clifton, Sylvia Turner. Front row: Linda Worthington, Olwyn Jacques, Venetia Blastock, Jacqueline Styche, -?-. The school was built in 1829 and demolished in 1966. *(Kath Lewis)*

The craft session has long been a favourite school pastime. This delightful study of some budding young artists was taken at Old Park Primary School, *c.* 1961. Far left is Sandra Bagley. *(Old Park Primary School)*

Old Park headmaster William Greenwood stands far right on the back row in a 1962 gathering in the school gymnasium. Back row, left to right: Derek Weeks, Michael Barratt, Lorraine Dawson, Susan Rowley, Christine Boucher, Ann Faulkner, Patrick Cotterill, Peter Murphy. Third row: Glen Darby, Alfred James, Peter Baxter, Colin Grice, John Page, -?-, Robert Turford, Clive Whitehouse, Arthur Foster. Second row: Christine Richards, Yvonne Bagnall, Carol Robinson, Janet Talbot, Linda Day, Miranda Holland, June Edwards, -?-. Front row: Kenneth Baker, Anthony Bradley, Peter Jenkins, Michael Howell, Raymond Dicken. *(Old Park Primary School)*

Old Park pupils experience the fun of staging their own puppet show, *c*. 1961. *(Old Park Primary School)*

Mayoress Mrs William Taylor tries her luck on the 'Kill The Rat' stall after officially opening Old Park School's summer fête in 1954. The three women standing directly behind are, left to right, June Shilton, Katherine Clarke, Maria Mullender. Old Park's fêtes were often organised by the town's Rotary Club, with headmaster William Greenwood being a Rotarian himself. *(Old Park Primary School)*

Kitchen and caretaking staff at Holyhead Road Senior Girls School, 1949. Built in 1933, the establishment changed its name to Heronville before a further change to its present title, Holyhead Road Primary. On the back row, second left, is caretaker Ted Spooner, while fourth left is Edie Hodgkins. *(Mike Horton)*

Old Park kitchen staff smile for the camera on a sunny day in 1962. Back row, left to right: -?-, Mrs Weeks, -?-, Mrs Pugh, Mrs Smith, -?-, Mrs Hodgkins. Front row: Mrs Hughes, Headmaster William Greenwood, -?-, Secretary Mrs Watts, -?-. *(Old Park Primary School)*

Above: The Mayor, Alderman Vic Steed, presents a winner's trophy at Wednesbury Boys High School athletics day, 5 July 1958. Established by strict headmaster Cyril Stanley Kipping in 1924, this celebrated institution was superseded by Wood Green High School in 1960 at its St Paul's Road address. *(Sue Jackson)*

School swimming galas were held at Walsall Street Baths on an annual basis. Here the Mayor, Councillor Leonard Waldron, presents a shield in 1961. Deputy headmistress of Holyhead Road Juniors, Stella Hill, stands second right with teacher Frederick Phipps far right. *(Diane Maynard)*

Winning smiles from St Bartholomew's boys swimming team in 1954 as they pose with competition shields in their Church Street schoolyard. Left to right: Leslie Flowers, John Heynes, -?-, Adrian ?, Malcolm Osbourne, Raymond Stokes. The shields were for best team and best school. *(Kath Lewis)*

Below: A Wednesbury Boys High School swimmer receives his prize from Mayor Alderman Vic Steed following the school's annual gala, held on 22 July 1958 at the Walsall Street Baths. *(Sue Jackson)*

Holyhead Road Senior Girls netball team join for a formal photograph during their 1950/1 season. Back row, left to right: Margaret Kennedy, teacher – Miss Constable, Sheila Kendrick. Front row: Beryl Kendrick, Joan Green, Sheila Perrin, Barbara Baker (captain), Brenda Wright, Norma Gould, Beryl Hughes. *(Norma Caswell)*

Footballers from Kings Hill County Secondary Boys School gather for a 1953/4 season photo shoot. Back row, left to right: G. Sawbridge, M. Hesson, R. Berry, H. Haddock, J. Casserley, H. Ball, R. White. Front row: L. Riley, T. Burns, S. Dugmore, A. Bagnall, D. Talbot, G. Moseley. *(Terry Burns)*

Pictured in front of the school sandpit are Old Park Primary football team, 1956/7. Players and teachers identified are: first row, second left, John Maybury; far right, Barry Turner; second row, third left, Michael Price; far right, Michael Langley; back row, left to right: deputy head Wilfred Slater, Alan Hollingsworth, headmaster William Greenwood. *(Old Park Primary School)*

Wodensborough High School, Hydes Road, perform their annual pantomime in December 1971. The stage set has been painted by highly talented artists. Pupil Kim Norridge is seventh left on the front row. Wodensborough was originally opened in September 1958 as the Wednesbury Girls High School. *(Doreen Pugh)*

Little is known about the above schoolroom, which stood in Walsall Street. Historian Frederick Hackwood describes it in 1884 as a private 'Higher Grade' school, under the principalship of a Mr Longstaffe MCP. The Ordnance Survey of 1888 shows it as a boys' school, but for many years it was the premises of the Wednesbury Laundry Co. Ltd. Seen here while demolition was in progress on 5 February 1967, the site is now built over with a 24-hour petrol station and supermarket development. *(Bernard Minton)*

This section of Holyhead Road Juniors, seen here in 1968, was actually sited at the lower end of Meeting Street. These buildings have been replaced with the Archer Close and Cinder Way residential streets. The church on the extreme right is St Bartholomew's. *(Freda Riley)*

2

Home Sweet Home

Wednesbury Corporation executed an extensive 'slum clearance' programme from 1935 onwards. One of its many clearance orders included the Dale Street area, such as nos 1–12, Court 1, as pictured above. A prominent sanitary evil was the open drain, seen running the length of the brick paved passageway. To the right are the shared 'brewhouses', identified by their tall chimneys, where communal laundering took place, usually on a Monday. *(Brian Broome)*

Close by Court 1 can be seen back-to-back houses 35 and 36 Dale Street, again in 1935. Accommodation in this type of premises was usually no more than 'two up two down'. The open door at the rear of the right-hand brewhouse reveals the basic lavatory, shared by both families of the front and back house. Replacement houses were built in 1949. (*Brian Broome*)

Drew's Court was situated off Lower High Street, opposite the Board School (now St John's Primary). The rear of nos 11 and 12 are pictured in 1935, showing the washday implements of wooden barrel and cast-iron mangle. Laundry would be agitated in the barrel's soapy water with a 'dolly' (which resembled a stool on a pole), while excess water would be squeezed from the washing through the mangle's wooden rollers. The tiny windows only allowed limited daylight to the often cramped living quarters. To the right, a hen scratches for food in the alleyway. (*Author's collection*)

This backyard scene at Trow's Square, off Portway Road, was typical of Wednesbury's poorer housing stock. Many such places were hurriedly constructed with little or no thought for social conditions and town planning, to meet housing demands for a rapidly expanding population during the latter years of the Industrial Revolution. Walls were often whitewashed (as seen here in 1933) to expose damp and mould. In the right foreground can just be seen a galvanised bucket alongside the single water tap, which would have been the only drinking supply for the surrounding households. (*Author's collection*)

The mixed variety of housing in Wellcroft Street can be seen in this 1936 photograph taken from St Bartholomew's belltower. Modern council houses with generous front gardens can be viewed in the left foreground, surrounded, in contrast, by older abodes whose front doors opened straight onto the street. (*Cyril Beardmore*)

Walton Road takes shape during construction of the Wednesbury side of the giant Friar Park housing estate in 1935. This view is towards the junction of Price Road with Walton Road, on land that was formerly fields belonging to Crankhall Farm. *(Sam Stevenson)*

The Wood Green housing estate was built between 1919 and 1922 on land conveyed from the Patent Shaft and Axletree Co. Ltd. Not much of the original windows or fencing survives today from this picture of a newly completed Hales Road. *(Author's collection)*

Myvod Road was laid out as part of the Park Lane estate in 1933. The name is derived from the village of Meifod, near Welshpool, which was one-time home to the industrious Lloyd family, who founded the former Lloyd's Steelworks at Wednesbury. Careful observation will reveal a streetlight engineer at work. *(Diane Maynard)*

Many of Wednesbury's inhabitants lived in close proximity to its sprawling industrial sites, such as Bannister Road, Leabrook, pictured in about 1970 in the shadow of the Patent Shaft Steelworks. *(Ken Smith)*

Little Annie Rowland stands at the open doorway to her home, Hobs Hole Farmhouse, at Banner's Farm, Wood Green, 1914. Many such rural retreats survived around Wednesbury until the First World War. The site of the farm is now built over with Jockey Lane. *(Annie Spittle)*

Below: Nos 13 and 14 Bridge Street were a once fine pair of Georgian houses that stood at the junction with Potter's Lane. In recent years no. 13 (left) served as office premises to G. & S. Lees Ltd, nut and bolt manufacturer, while no. 14 was home to Wednesbury Rugby Football Club. Pictured here in about 1970, both were demolished in May 2002. *(Black Country Society)*

Combeford Cottage, Bridge Street, was the Wednesbury home of the celebrated local historian Frederick William Hackwood. The frontage of the neatly kept residence is pictured (to the left) in 1897, while the view to the rear of the property (right) shows the effects of mining subsidence in 1899. This was caused by a subterranean fire in the workings of the nearby Mounts Colliery, an occurrence known locally as 'wildfire'. *(Author's collection)*

Brunswick Park Lodge, Wood Green Road, adjacent to the original entrance gates, 1915. The lodge dates from 1887 and was built to the original design of William Barron, of Borrowash, Derbyshire, who landscaped the park's 28 acres of pleasure grounds, opened on 21 June that year by the Mayor Alderman Richard Williams JP, to celebrate the Golden Jubilee of Queen Victoria. *(Author's collection)*

The little girl with handmuff, standing at the entrance gates to Oakeswell Hall in about 1910, is probably one of the nine children of surgeon Dr Walter Garman, the then occupier. One of his daughters, Lorna, married Ernest Wishart of Sussex, their son Michael (1928–96) becoming a famous artist and writer. Her sister Kathleen married the sculptor Sir Jacob Epstein in 1955, her name immortalised in the Garman Ryan collection of Epstein's works at the New Art Gallery, Walsall. The lantern tower among the tall chimneys was an unusual feature of the hall. To the right is a rare view of the rear of the ancient building, 22 July 1961. *(Kitty Godley)*

Oakeswell Hall's entrance parlour is pictured in 1957, the view through the window being to its boundary wall along Walsall Street. Noticeable are the carved ceiling timbers, half-panelled walls and stained glass window in the entrance door. Regrettably, the hall – first mentioned in 1421 – was demolished in 1962. *(Wolverhampton Express & Star)*

Another historical mansion house in Wednesbury was The Hollies, which stood opposite Oakeswell Hall at the top of Hollies Drive, where Georgian Gardens residential development now stands. Seen here in December 1952, it was built in about 1820 by Mr Whitmore Jones, owner of Wednesbury Mill, and was once the home of James Russell of tubemaking fame. The Hollies was demolished in about 1970. (*Wolverhampton Express & Star*)

The oak timber frames of Tudor houses, 25 to 28 High Bullen, are exposed during demolition for the Northern Orbital Bypass in 1969. Located at a spot known as Hancox Green in medieval times, they were latterly occupied as shops by Glaze's antiques, Webb's tobacconist and Horton's corn merchants. (*Bernard Minton*)

Wednesbury Labour MP John Stonehouse performs the opening ceremony at Queens Gardens and Kings Court housing development, 9 May 1964. Mr Stonehouse (far right) was returned as Parliamentary representative for the town on 28 February 1957. Joining him from left are Mayor Councillor Mark Allen, -?-, Mrs Allen, Barbara Stonehouse, Chairman of the housing committee Alderman Vic Steed. *(Norman Pearson)*

Queens Gardens from the Holyhead Road, 1965. The flats offered new residents the luxuries of landscaped grounds, lifts, a community room, inside toilets and fitted kitchens. The wooden stagecoach mural on the gable end commemorates Thomas Telford's improvement of the London to Holyhead coaching route through Wednesbury in 1826. It has now been restored and resited at nearby Holyhead Road Primary School, much to the credit of headmistress Hilary Bills, Councillor Frank Betteridge, David Humphries, Joe Davies, Charlotte Davies, Vicky Bliss and Wednesbury Civic Society. Queens Gardens and Kings Court were demolished in 2002. *(Ken Smith)*

3

A Royal Welcome

The people of Wednesbury played host to Her Majesty Queen Elizabeth II on the
occasion of her visit to the borough on Thursday 24 May 1962. Residents and
local school pupils eagerly await the royal motorcade outside St Paul's church,
Wood Green Road – en route from an earlier visit to Walsall.
(Diane Maynard)

Crowds gather in Holyhead Road with union jacks at the ready. All the local schoolchildren were allowed time off lessons to greet the royal visitor. *(Diane Maynard)*

Police Superintendent I.R. Cogbill instructs a motorcycle patrol officer as more policemen line the route. The church of St John's can be seen to the right. *(Author's collection)*

The welcoming party gathers at the Town Hall
entrance. Left to right: Town Clerk George
Frederick Thompson, Mayoress Hannah
Waldron, Mayor Councillor Leonard Waldron
and mace bearer Bruce Bennett. *(Diane Maynard)*

The Mayor's granddaughter, six-year-old Diane
Waldron, practises her curtsey prior to
presenting the Queen with a floral posy on
arrival. *(Diane Maynard)*

An ecstatic crowd erupts in cheering and flag-waving as the monarch arrives in a gleaming Rolls-Royce Phantom V. *(Author's collection)*

The Queen is greeted by the Mayor as the Lord Lieutenant of Staffordshire, H. Wallace Copland, looks on. To the left of the group is the Lady-in-Waiting, the Countess Euston.
(Diane Maynard)

Her Royal Highness takes her seat
on the Town Hall stage, surrounded
by councillors, clergy and officials.
The table and chair provided seem
rather plain for such an important
visitor and special occasion.
(Diane Maynard)

The Mayor, Councillor Leonard
Waldron, witnesses as the Queen
signs a portrait photograph of
herself. The leather handbag on her
arm was almost certainly made in
nearby Walsall by Launer and Co.
(Diane Maynard)

The Mayor and Mayoress present the Queen with a copy of the *History of Wednesbury*. In the background can be seen, left to right: Councillor John Henry O'Neil, Alderman Ethel Price, Alderman Vic Steed, the Revd John Talbot. *(Diane Maynard)*

A close up of the specially leather-bound copy of the *History of Wednesbury* presented to the Queen. Published by Wednesbury Corporation in 1962, following seven years' research, it was written by John Frederick Ede MA, the history master at Wednesbury Boys High School. The cover is embossed with the municipal coat of arms, granted in 1904. The crest, a tower in flames, represents a blast furnace and is taken from the coat of arms belonging to the Hopkins family, who resided at Oakeswell Hall during the Civil War. The rising sun behind signifies a new dawn in the town's history. On the shield, the two heraldic lions are from the coat of arms of the Heronville family, twelfth-century Lords of the Manor. At the centre, the fesse portrays two sable lozenges, representing black diamonds, otherwise coal, between which is the symbol of Mars, denoting the iron and steel trades. Below, the Latin motto, *Arte, Marte, Vigore*, translates to 'By Skill, By Iron, By Energy'. The Latin '*Marte*' is also a reference to the town's obsolete gun trade. *(Diane Maynard)*

A press photographer claims a prime position to photograph the royal visitor as she joins the Town Clerk and Mayor on the Town Hall balcony. Rather amusingly, this appearance was unplanned and various domestic items and rubbish had been stored on the balcony 'out of sight'! *(Diane Maynard)*

Below: The Queen crosses the red carpet to the waiting royal car after being bade farewell by the Mayor outside the Town Hall. Nurses from Moxley Isolation Hospital gain an unobstructed view of the departing royal visitor. *(Diane Maynard)*

A short drive away from the Town Hall was Wednesbury Central station on the Great Western line, at which the Queen caught the Royal Train to leave the Midlands. Here she shakes hands with Bram Dunn, the newly appointed stationmaster. *(Bram Dunn)*

Below: The Queen returns a beaming smile as she takes the salute from the Lord Lieutenant, while the Royal Train pulls out of Wednesbury station, thus bringing a glorious occasion for the town to an end. *(Diane Maynard)*

4

Mesty Croft Memories

Although much of the old Mesty Croft was developed from the 1850s onwards, some
buildings pre-dating this time still survived well into the twentieth century. One such property
was the Red House, which was of late Georgian appearance and situated between
St Luke's Road and the South Staffordshire railway line. When pictured, sometime during
the First World War, the older and invalided menfolk worked its grounds as allotments.
Red House Avenue was built in its adjoining paddock in about 1950.
The Red House was listed as the residence of J. Hughes in 1953; it has since
been demolished. *(Dorothy Hill)*

Mesty Croft Board School was built in 1880 also to serve the adjoining parish of Wood Green. Only a few pupils in this 1925 photograph can be identified. Second row, third left: Mary Parker. Front row, left to right: Lily Bushell, Evelyn Smith, Vera Bayley, -?-. *(Malcolm P. Turner)*

Percussion instruments are held at the ready as the conductor raises her baton in this posed composition of 1937 in front of the new school extension. *(Bill Day)*

Headmaster Mr Sandham (left) and physical education teacher Mr Hunter join the school football team for their official 1949/50 season photograph. Back row, left to right: E. Dicken, D. Harper, G. Norton, T. Wood, A. Bates, A. Eagles, M. Jones, A. Dunn. Front row: P. Blastock, C. Partridge, V. Webb, T. Burns, H. Humphries. *(Terry Burns)*

The newly laid Hydes Road playing fields were the venue for Mesty Croft school sports day in 1956. Officially opened on 31 August by Mayor Councillor John Edwin James, they occupy 21 acres given by the Patent Shaft and Axletree Co. The young runners awaiting 'starters orders' are, left to right, Jean Myatt, Susan Archer, Janet Robinson, Kathleen Peasley, Susan Rosewarne and Eileen Millard. In the distance the spire of St John's church rises above Woden Road South. One of the cooling towers of Ocker Hill power station can be seen on the horizon, extreme left. *(Sue Mills)*

Mothers gather to encourage their children's sporting achievements, again at Hydes Road, 1957. Back row, left to right, -?-, -?-, Doris Beardmore, Joan Whitehouse, Mrs Derry, Hilda Archer. The embankment in the background carries the Tame Valley canal of 1844. *(Sue Mills)*

Numbered competitors smile for the camera, also in 1957. It will be observed that the trees that now grow in abundance on the bar of land separating Hydes Road pool from the River Tame and playing fields have not yet been planted. *(Sue Mills)*

Mesty Croft War Memorial committee gather in front of the village's monument to their fallen, *c.* 1947. The old school buildings – in whose grounds the memorial still stands – were replaced by modern classrooms in the 1980s. Back row, left to right: Jack Chambers, Charles Muckley, George Small, -?-, Frank Wilson, Jack Carless. Front row: -?-, Ivy May, Elsie Allen, -?-, Nancy James. The monument was sculpted by Wednesbury stonemasons Isaac Hill and Sons of Walsall Street. A dedication stone was laid by the tubemaker James McDougall on 10 July 1920. It was first unveiled by Alderman A.E. Pritchard JP, CC on 28 August 1920 and – following the Second World War – re-unveiled by Captain E.C. Pritchard MC on 26 July 1946. *(Dorothy Hill)*

These brave Mesty Croft men from the Fowell and Clymer families proudly gather in heroic pose, following their safe return from the First World War. Those who sacrificed their lives for King and country are remembered on the war memorial as follows.

First World War, 1914–18:
Pte W. Bradshaw, S. Hall, I. Kendrick, J.T. Tibbs, E. Wilkes, J.H. Chambers, I. Farnsworth, H. Severn, C. Spittle, W. Constable, J. Thomas, H. Clarke, J. Plant, Sgt J.W. Fisher, Sgt J. Gibbons, Cpl W. Styles, Pte S. Mason, 2nd Lt A.H. Adams, 2nd Lt S. Walters, Coy Sgt Maj J. Hayward, Sgt A. Wilkes, Sgt H. Bates, Sgt N. Beesley, Cpl A.E. Plant, Lce Cpl H. Thomas, Sig E.H. Smith RN, ERA G. Bourne RN, Sap B. Bartle, Driver A. Norton, Pte W.E. Henderson, Pte W. Hill, Pte J. Johnson, Pte C. Cherrington, Pte F. Neale, Pte B. Moseley, Pte E. Reeves.

Second World War, 1939–45:
Pte J. Worthington, Pte J. Thickett, Pte W.E. Churchill, Pte W.E. Cooper, Pte L. Price, Pte J. May, AB J. Hunt RN, Sap F. Ingram, Trp J. Dent, Gnr S.T. Scott, Rfl F.W. Aston, LAC W. Beardsmore, AB L. Jellyman RN. *(Sid Clymer)*

The wartime Mesty Croft Auxiliary Fire Service volunteers are gathered before their second annual dinner in 1941. Second right on the front row is Len Westley, who was chauffeur for the McDougall family, whose tubeworks stood opposite his home in Elwell Street. George McDougall is seated fifth from the right, also on the front row. *(Brian Broome)*

Victory in Europe Day, 1945, was celebrated with street parties across the nation. One such event was at Paul Street, where the buffet table – seen far left – was set up outside W.H. Eagles' grocery store. Third left, a sailor joins in the land-locked celebrations to mark the end of the Second World War. *(Author's collection)*

Pictured at the rear of the Green Dragon, Market Place, are Brookside Rangers FC, who were celebrating winning Division II of the Wednesbury League, 1949/50 season. Back row, left to right: Ivor Bache, Bill Day, Bill Burbridge, Ron Jones, Stan Lawrence, Horace Dawes, Green Dragon licensee Billy Hawkes. Front row: Jimmy Longmore, Les Smith, George Davies, Albert Kemp, Howard Meredith, Les Rogers. Brookside is that part of Mesty Croft closest to the River Tame. *(Bill Day)*

Residents and town councillors board a robust-looking vehicle in 1958. Those seen in the foreground are, left to right, -?-, Mayor Alderman Vic Steed, Alderman George Price, Mayoress Henrietta Maude Steed, Councillor George Stokes, the Revd Walter Thomas Sidwell, -?-. Mr Sidwell was vicar of St Luke's, Mesty Croft, for twelve years, until his sad death in January 1965 aged eighty-eight. *(Sue Jackson)*

The original St Luke's church stood in Alma Street, on land between St Luke's Road and Red House Avenue. Divine services began in 1881 in what had previously been a charity school, administered by the Elwell family of Wednesbury Forge since 1874. The church is seen here in 1972 when a rebuilding fund was steadily accumulating, as evident from the 'fundometer' attached to the outside wall. *(Gladys Steventon)*

St Luke's chancel was added to the original building in 1885. Here, the interior is shown in 1929. The old church has now been demolished following the consecration of a new St Luke's on 26 March 1974, in nearby Elwell Street. *(Gladys Steventon)*

Elwell Street Wesley chapel, which came under the Spring Head circuit, was built in 1862 to administer the faith to Mesty Croft's followers of Methodism. The chapel is pictured in its centenary year – 1962. *(Sam Stevenson)*

Below: Worshippers are seen at Wesley chapel's annual prize-giving service, 1952. Mesty Croft amalgamated with Spring Head when the new Central Mission was opened on 9 March 1968. The old chapel, which stood on the corner of Sampson Street, has since been demolished. *(Jean Simmons)*

Mesty Croft Wesleyans return to their chapel – along Elwell Street – during the 1952 anniversary parade. The second building from the top of the road is no. 9, M. Willies' general store. This is where the new St Luke's church now stands. Beyond can be seen the newly built houses of Red House Avenue. *(Jean Simmons)*

Jovial 'Newtowners' don fancy dress and equip themselves with collecting tins during the 1956 annual carnival. The name New Town was coined when much of Mesty Croft was developed by the shareholders of the Wednesbury Benefit Building Society in the 1850s. Those in fancy dress are, left to right, Winnie Cox, Jack Price, Bill Price, Elsie Garner, Gladys Cox and Mary ?. The little boy, far left, is Billy Noon. *(Gladys Cox)*

The children of Moor Street were treated to an open air party to celebrate the coronation of Queen Elizabeth II on 2 June 1953. Together with Richard Williams Road, Kilvert Road, Oxford Terrace and part of Hackwood Road, Moor Street was laid out in 1928. *(Gladys Cox)*

Victory in Europe Day, 1945, is marked with a street party by the residents of Kilvert Road. Its name commemorates Alderman John Ashley Kilvert JP, Mayor in 1905–6, who served in the 'Charge of the Light Brigade' during the Crimean War. *(Les Smith)*

Members of the Wednesbury Fellowship of the Disabled sort jumble before a fundraising sale at the Mesty Croft Darby & Joan Memorial Hall, 6 September 1964. The fellowship was formed in March 1960 to support the needs of the town's disabled residents. *(Norma Caswell)*

Mesty Croft's Darby & Joan Memorial Hall was opened on land off Oxford Street by Alderman George Wilson Price JP in January 1957. This well-known landmark was burnt to the ground exactly forty years later in an arson attack on New Year's Day 1997. *(Author's collection)*

Mesty Croft signal-box was located where the London and North Western railway (otherwise known as the South Staffordshire line) crossed Crankhall Lane at its junction with Oldbury Street and Brunswick Park Road. Seen here in 1968, the line has since closed to rail traffic and the box has long been dismantled. *(Black Country Society)*

Named after a Polish nobleman, the Mazeppa Inn stood at the bottom of Elwell Street at its junction with Friar Street and Brookside. The inn, pictured in 1968, survived large-scale redevelopment of Mesty Croft during the late 1960s and later became the offices of Wharfdale Steels Ltd. Its own end came on 28 April 1997 to make way for a works car park. *(Alan Price)*

WEDNESBURY BOROUGH ELECTIONS, 1955
(MESTY CROFT WARD)

Mrs. Margaret Burkitt

(Your Conservative Candidate)

Asks for your support
when you go to Vote on

Polling Day Thursday, May 12th

8.0 a.m. to 9.0 p.m.

YOU VOTE AT — MESTY CROFT SCHOOLS (T)

Committee Rooms—Mrs. Palmer, 15 Piercy Street, Wednesbury.

Published by Mr. G. F. Liddy, Conservative Offices, Walsall Street, Wednesbury
Printed by Robert Riley, Russell Street, Wednesbury

Conservative candidate Mrs Margaret Burkitt stood for Mesty Croft ward during the Wednesbury Borough Elections of 12 May 1955. Votes were cast at Mesty Croft school, which rewarded pupils with an extra day's leave from class. Piercy Street, the address of the committee rooms, no longer exists. *(Paul Burkitt)*

Municipal Election

**Thursday
8th
May**

SAM

STEVENSON

Deserves Your
Support

Labour opposition often came in the shape of much respected former Town Councillor Sam Stevenson JP. Here he contests a seat on West Bromwich County Borough Council after the amalgamation with Wednesbury in 1966. Mr Stevenson was first voted on to Wednesbury Council in 1954 and – though retired – is an active and very popular Mesty Croft resident to this day. *(Sam Stevenson)*

5

Trading Places

Wednesbury Market Place is anciently the principal trading centre of the town, resplendent since 1911 with its handsome clock tower, erected to mark the Coronation of King George V. The shops seen at the centre of this 1949 photograph, nos 26a, 26 and 26b, then trading as Disturnal's grocers, Riley stationers and Benefit footwear were once joined as one complete townhouse, as described in the manorial court rolls of 1786. A document dated 1861 mentions the division of the property into three separate shops. Recently two of the units have been reunited as Simon's News in what are possibly the oldest surviving buildings in the town centre today. *(Alan Price)*

An open-air market was held on this spot long before Queen Anne granted its royal charter in 1709, at which time a brick Market Cross building stood, similar to those that survive at Bridgnorth and Ross-on-Wye. This was pulled down in 1824. This photograph was taken on 11 August 1968. To the left of the clock tower, the box-like upper floor of 22 Market Place, formerly Taylors bakery, was removed on 26 March 1989. This property is another strong contender for the title of the town centre's oldest building. *(Alan Price)*

The canvas weather sheeting – as seen above Hodgetts fruiterers and greengrocers – offered only rudimentary protection from the elements. Hodgetts trade at Wednesbury Market to this day. Nos 1 to 5 Market Place, visible in this picture of July 1965, were demolished in February 1989, and the new Jobcentre at Woden House opened on the site in 1993. *(Ken Smith)*

Bargain hunting proves hot work for one lady on a sunny market day in July 1965. The ancient Market Rights were sold by the Scott and Foley families, joint Lords of the Manor to the Wednesbury Board of Health, in 1861. These were adopted by Wednesbury Corporation on its creation in 1886. *(Ken Smith)*

Councillors and Town Hall staff took on the task of erecting market stalls during a Public Works Dept strike in 1955. Left to right: Betty Brown, Councillor Edward Noel Chorley, Ann Hollingsworth. The weekly market, held on Fridays and Saturdays, was removed to a purpose-built covered site in the nearby Shambles in 1970. This in turn is due to be swept away for a massive hypermarket development. *(Ann Betteridge)*

Alfred Stiles, 'Complete Home Furnishers', 33 Upper High Street, 1914. The extensive array of goods on display includes bedsteads, dining chairs, occasional tables, trunks and pushchairs. The premises are still recognisable today, although now occupied by a ladies' hairdresser. *(Author's collection)*

Dispensing chemist David Jackson stands in the entrance to his original pharmacy at 169 Holyhead Road, in 1909. The business was later transferred to no. 72, with a branch also in Walsall Street. *(Author's collection)*

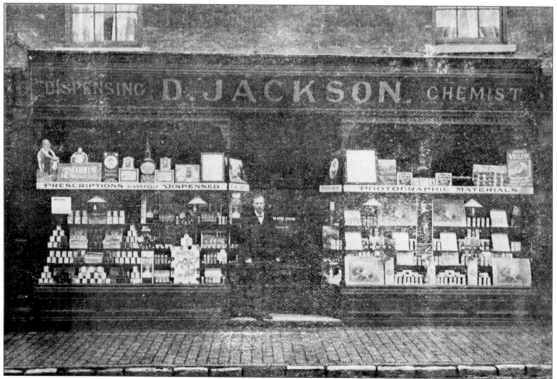

Tailor George Powell joins staff at 19 Market Place for this excellent study, *c.* 1919. The patriotic sandwich board urges the public to 'Keep buying, keep the flag flying!' Far left, a four-legged friend decides to pose, too. In the 1920s F.W. Woolworth and Co. Ltd built their new Wednesbury store on the site. *(Mary Burkitt)*

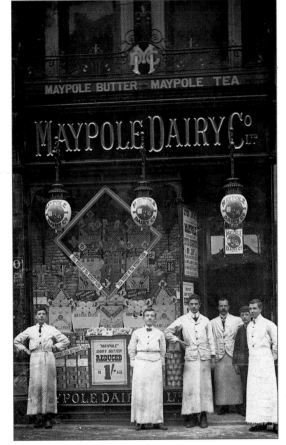

Dressing the Maypole Dairy Co.'s window, at 16 Market Place, must have been an arduous task for its staff, pictured here in their shop overalls in 1907. Freshly churned butter was bought on an almost daily basis before widespread affordable domestic refrigeration arrived in the 1950s. *(Author's collection)*

Saleswoman Sally Wedgbury at Edith Minett's ladies outfitters, 83 Walsall Street, *c.* 1938. At about this time an extra showroom had been created out of part of the neighbouring Taylor's garage premises. *(Brenda Greenhough)*

Minett's and the adjacent hair salon of Bert Hemmings were patriotically dressed up for the coronation of George VI, 12 May 1937. Ice-cream salesman G. Chiloni was probably heading towards nearby Brunswick Park with his handcart in anticipation of a roaring trade. E. Minett still clothes Wednesbury's best-dressed ladies today from behind its unspoilt art deco shopfront. *(Brenda Greenhough)*

Optician J.H. Robbins grinds a
spectacle lens in his practice at
1a Union Street, 1936. To his
side can be seen his assistant,
Mrs Booth. The business was
established in 1911, later
moving to no. 26 before crossing
the road to more modern
premises, and still trades in
Union Street today. A timetable
of train services from
Wednesbury adorns the wall
while below a chalked notice
reads 'Test here 2 o'clock and at
Darlaston 3.30 tomorrow'.
(Ann Betteridge)

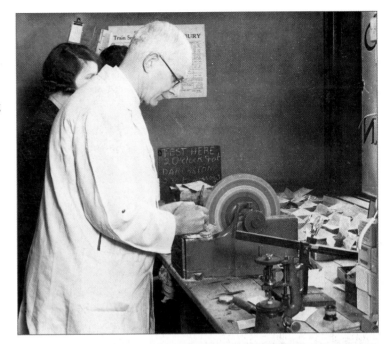

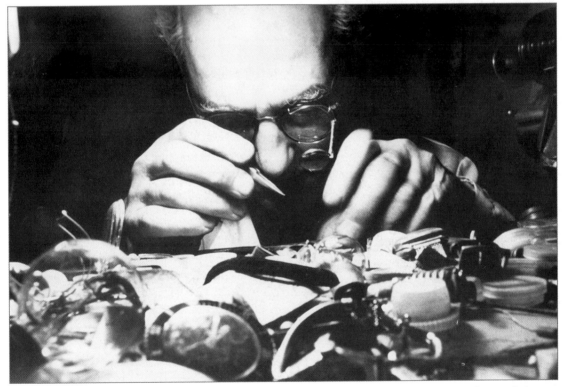

Wednesbury horologist Joseph Leslie Beardmore focuses on another wristwatch repair in his workshop at
31 Upper High Street, 1976. Self-taught, he hand-wound St Bartholomew's church clock every week for
forty-eight years from 1928 until 1976. Other public timepieces he maintained were at St Paul's, St
John's and All Saints' (Moxley) churches, as well as the Coronation Clock Tower, Market Place and the
pillar clock in Brunswick Park. The photographs of Wellcroft Street (page 21) and Church Street (page
80) were taken by Mr Beardmore from the belltower of St Bartholomew's church. *(Cyril Beardmore)*

Typical of many 'front room' neighbourhood shops was 1 Dale Street, kept by Jabez and Eliza Burgess. Before being fitted out with a counter and shelving, the front room would have been family living accommodation. The shop was included in the slum clearance order of 1936. *(Brian Broome)*

Below: Street corners were favourite trading locations. Thomas Berry's grocery store was situated at 37 Addison Street, on its corner with Addison Terrace. The proprietor was also a well-known Wednesbury councillor, serving as Mayor in 1953–4. Cherry Blossom shoe polish is advertised in this 1950s picture. This fine traditional establishment was pulled down in 1966. *(Albert Wassall)*

Above: Henry Hollingsworth established his Wednesbury butchering dynasty in 1857. Postwar expansion saw the business develop its wholesale operations from purpose-built premises in Camp Street. Daily deliveries were made to independent butchers in surrounding districts, using a fleet of Thames 1500 commercial vans in olive-green and yellow livery, as seen here in about 1965. The delivery van's registration plate would command a fair price today! *(Ann Betteridge)*

Grocery delivery boy Alan Jinks prepares to set off with fully laden bicycle, from the forecourt of Walsall and District Co-operative branch no. 56, situated in Crankhall Lane, opposite the Brunswick Inn. This early 1960s picture reminds us of a once much-favoured and cost-effective form of delivery, often also employed by the local butcher and baker. *(Sue Mills)*

The office of the *Midland Advertiser* and *Wednesbury Borough News* was situated at 48 Lower High Street, where these two – now extinct – newspapers were published and sold. Pictured in about 1970, the premises stand at the junction with Addison Terrace and are now occupied by a Chinese takeaway. *(Black Country Society)*

Below: Holloway's toyshop, at 44 and 45 Lower High Street, was an Aladdin's cave for generations of Wednesbury boys and girls. The premises – seen here in about 1979 – are now a kitchen showroom. *(Ken Smith)*

An 1834 directory states that 'In 1816, Mr Richard Woolrich erected, on one side of the Market Place, a small butchers' market consisting of two rows of shops'. This was the earliest reference to Wednesbury's Shambles. This view from the Shambles to its junction with Camp Street shows, on the right, the 1908 former engine house to Wednesbury Corporation's electricity generating works, established in 1904. Today the premises are occupied by the busy and very popular R.J. Discount Warehouse. Also seen in the picture – dated 1 February 1967 – is the Jolly Brewer public house, Camp Street, which was demolished in 1970. *(Bernard Minton)*

Lola (left) and Maggie O'Connell eagerly await customers for their apples, priced 8*d* per pound, and lemons, two for 6*d*, at Matt O'Connell's fruiterers, 27 and 28 Union Street, in 1948. This long-established family business still supplies Wednesbury's healthy eaters today. *(Bridget Coles)*

Alfred Cartwright's cafeteria, 36 and 37 Union Street, stood at the junction with High Bullen, Dudley Street and Camphill Lane until its demolition in 1976. This photograph of about 1955 also shows – far left – the traffic lights which controlled the once busy crossroads. *(Author's collection)*

The junction of Union Street with Upper High Street, 8 June 1969. The wooden booth outside the George Inn was a sales pitch for the *Express & Star* evening newspaper. Across the road the vacant plot in Upper High Street was formerly occupied by the Grapes public house, demolished two years earlier. *(Mike Horton)*

6

Civic Pride

Wednesbury Corporation elected forty-five different mayors during its eighty-year lifespan between 1886 and 1966. Some held office more than once and one, Sir Albert Pritchard, served the town five times. The Mayoral Election is seen here on 27 May 1961. To the left, Town Clerk George Frederick Thompson reads from the Declaration of the Acceptance of Office, while the newly elected Mayor, Councillor Leonard Waldron, prepares to take the Oath of Allegiance. In the foreground is the silver-gilt mace, presented by Alderman Richard Williams JP, first Mayor of Wednesbury in 1886–7 and again in 1887–8. *(Diane Maynard)*

Mayor (1958–9) Alderman Vic Steed makes his acceptance speech on the Town Hall stage. He is flanked by the Town Clerk and Councillor Walter Morgan, who was the outgoing mayor. The Mayor's chain of office, made of eighteen-carat gold, was purchased by public subscription in 1886. *(Sue Jackson)*

The occasion of the Mayoral Election was during each Annual General Meeting of the council, held every May at the Town Hall. Wednesbury's Member of Parliament, John Stonehouse, is pictured fifth left at the 1958 AGM, while his wife, Barbara, sits alongside between their two young daughters. *(Sue Jackson)*

Wednesbury's only lady mayor was Alderman Ethel Price, who held office in 1950–1 and again – as seen here – in 1962–3. The councillors are pictured in the council chamber. Back row, left to right: -?-, George Carter, Norman Small, Jack Butler, Kenneth Henderson, Deputy Surveyor George Humphries, Harry Ashby, Roland Vernon, Jack Percival, John Edwin James, Arthur Rawlings, Borough Surveyor A.W. Ewart, William Griffiths, Deputy Mayor Sam Stevenson, Health Inspector Mr Turner, Albert Diggett, Deputy Treasurer Mr Tyler. Front row: Alderman Arthur Bissell, Alderman Vic Steed, Alderman George Price, Mayor Ethel Price, Town Clerk George Frederick Thompson, Thomas Berry, Leonard Waldron, Mark Allen. Mace bearer Bruce Bennett stands to the rear below a replica of HMS *Albrighton's* badge, the warship that was 'adopted' by Wednesbury Borough in 1942. *(Birmingham Post and Evening Mail)*

Councillors make their way past the derelict St Bartholomew's School in Church Street on the return journey from St Bartholomew's church to the Town Hall, following the annual Mayor's Sunday service in 1964. Excluding uniformed police, those pictured left to right are Arthur Rawlings, John Edwin James, Sam Stevenson, Roland Vernon, James Ralph, William Grifffiths, H. Astbury, Kenneth Henderson, Jack Stokes, Mark Allen, Albert Diggett, Alderman Vic Steed, James Turley, Alderman Ethel Price, Bill Westwood, Town Clerk George Frederick Thompson, Mace bearer Bruce Bennett, Mayor John Henry O'Neil, the Revd Peter Gerald Owen. *(Jack Stokes)*

Locals gather to watch the Mayor's Sunday parade cross the Five Ways junction in the town centre, 1956. Those seen in the foreground are, left to right, -?-, Town Clerk George Frederick Thompson, Mayor John Edwin James, Canon Alexander Bannerman Lavelle. Five Ways is so called because it is the junction of the Market Place with Union Street, Upper High Street, Church Street and Walsall Street. *(Sue Mills)*

Mace bearer Bruce Bennett leads the Mayor's Sunday parade up Church Street on 7 June 1959. He is closely followed by, left to right, Town Clerk George Frederick Thompson, Mayor George Stokes, the Revd Thomas Grimsdale Kelsey. *(Jack Stokes)*

The parade for Mayor's Sunday, 28 May 1961, passes the George and Dragon Hotel and Barclays Bank in Lower High Street. Starting with Town Clerk George Frederick Thompson, the line-up continues, left to right, -?-, Mayor Leonard Waldron, the Revd John Talbot, Mace bearer Bruce Bennett, Alderman Ethel Price, Alderman Vic Steed, Mark Allen, Arthur Rawlings, Thomas Berry. *(Sue Mills)*

The 1961 parade completes its circuit in Holyhead Road, with only yards to go to the Town Hall. Superintendent I.R. Cogbill leads the way, representing the local police force. Other organisations which took part in this annual event included the 5th Battalion South Staffs Regiment, 240 Squadron Air Training Corps, British Legion, Fire Brigade, Red Cross, Civil Defence Corps, St John Ambulance Brigade, Scouts, and Boys' and Girls' Brigades. Following steadily behind is a Walsall Corporation bus on the no. 38 circular route. *(Diane Maynard)*

John Henry O'Neil, Mayor in 1964, walks before the Revd Peter Gerald Owen, nearing St Bartholomew's church. The route from the Town Hall to church usually followed the Holyhead Road, Lower High Street, Market Place and Church Street. The vicar was known as the Mayor's Chaplain. *(Tony Mallam)*

The last Mayor of Wednesbury, Arthur Wallace Rawlings, ascends the steps to St Bartholomew's churchyard on Sunday 23 May 1965. The Mayor's robes were a gift of Alderman Wilson Lloyd JP, during his second term of office in 1900. The correct title for Mace bearer Bruce Bennett was Mayor's Sergeant. Standing between him and the Mayor is Special Constable Tony Mallam, who today dons a very different uniform in his role of Town Crier. *(Tony Mallam)*

Councillors and officials join the Mayor, Leonard Waldron, to remember Wednesbury's 'fallen' at the cenotaph, Walsall Street, on 12 November 1961. The war memorial grounds were dedicated in 1926. *(Diane Maynard)*

Republic of India Day is celebrated with a social evening at the Town Hall, 24 January 1959. In these postwar times many immigrants of varied ethnic cultures have harmoniously made Wednesbury their new home. Front row, left to right: John Stonehouse MP, -?-, Mayor Alderman Vic Steed, -?-, -?-, Mayoress Henrietta Maude Steed, Alderman George Price, Alderman Ethel Price, -?-, -?-. *(Sue Jackson)*

The Municipal Offices and Richards Art Gallery, *c.* 1900. The Municipal Offices – incorporating the Town Hall – were built by the Wednesbury Board of Health in 1871. This building was enlarged and remodelled in 1913 to create the Town Hall familiar to us today. The adjoining Art Gallery and Museum was opened 4 November 1891, the legacy of Mary Ann Richards (d. 1885) in memory of her late husband Edwin Richards (1820–80), coach axle manufacturer, of The Limes, Wood Green Road. The impressive terracotta façade is the work of Victorian sculptor George Tinworth, and features – at its centre – the busts of Alderman Richard Williams and Alderman Wilson Lloyd, the first two Mayors of Wednesbury. *(Author's collection)*

The Richards Room, Wednesbury Art Gallery, 1906. Most of the collection had been built up by Edwin Richards, growing with further donations in successive years. Over 355 works of art were catalogued in 1930. Astonishingly, it was reported in *The Times* on 24 April 1948 that an auction of 300 lots was to be held, to raise funds for the newly formed Society of Arts. Paintings by old masters such as R.S. Bond, James Webb and Eugene Verboeckhoven sold for as little as £25! Despite this, an excellent collection of artworks remain on view to the public today. *(Author's collection)*

Wednesbury's old library used to stand alongside the original baths in Walsall Street at its junction with Brunswick Terrace. The facility was opened in 1878 by Richard Williams, then Chairman of the Local Board of Health. It was demolished in 1912 and replaced with new education offices (see overleaf). *(Author's collection)*

The 'new' library was built further along Walsall Street in 1908, the gift of industrialist Andrew Carnegie, who witnessed experiments with the 'Basic Open-Hearth' steelmaking process in Wednesbury and used this knowledge to make a fortune in America. The main entrance in Hollies Drive is seen here from across the War Memorial Gardens in about 1930. *(Brian Beasley)*

The public baths, originally opened in 1878, were reconstructed to include new education offices and reopened on 18 July 1913 in a ceremony performed by the Mayor, Alderman Albert Pritchard. The handsome building – with its Matlock stone dressings – was closed in April 1973 and demolished soon afterwards. *(Author's collection)*

Facilities at the baths included two swimming pools with diving board and water chute, alongside eighteen slipper baths. The first-class pool, measuring 75ft × 28ft, is shown in 1913. New baths were opened in nearby Dudley Street on 30 March 1974. *(Author's collection)*

Mayoress Henrietta Maude Steed looks on as the Mayor, Alderman Vic Steed, presents St John Ambulance Brigade members with a competition trophy, 1 February 1959. The ambulancemen are, left to right, Richard Cadman, -?-, Herbert Davies, Sergeant Sidney Woodcock. *(Sue Jackson)*

The Mayor and Mayoress are joined by fellow members of the Association of Civic Heads for a tour of Edward Elwell Ltd, edge tool manufacturers, at Wednesbury Forge, St Paul's Road, 19 March 1959. The Mayoress' chain was given by Councillor John Knowles JP during his second term of office in 1900–1. *(Sue Jackson)*

Pensioners greet the Mayor, Alderman Vic Steed, while collecting Christmas gift bonuses in December 1958. *(Sue Jackson)*

Mrs Holland of 16 Harewood Avenue is served dinner by the Mayor, Alderman Vic Steed, during the inauguration of the Meals on Wheels service, 16 April 1959. Looking on are Alderman Arthur Bissell and the Mayoress, Henrietta Maude Steed. *(Sue Jackson)*

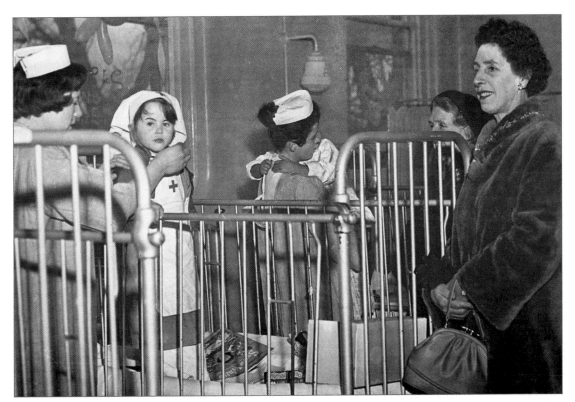

Mayoress Henrietta Maude Steed, far right, makes a Christmas Day visit to child patients at Moxley Infectious Diseases Isolation Hospital in 1958. One little girl is helped to dress in her new play nurse uniform. Out of a total of eighty-seven patients that day, seventy-five were under five years of age. In the evening patients and nursing staff were entertained by St Bartholomew's choir, conducted by Mr Gurney Harper. The lady left of the Mayoress, obscured by the cot, is Mrs Frank Baker, wife of the chairman of Darlaston Urban District Council. *(Sue Jackson)*

Portland House Maternity Hospital, Wood Green Road, is the scene of this Christmas Day visit in 1961. To the left are the Mayoress, Hannah Waldron, and Mayor, Leonard Waldron. *(Diane Maynard)*

Left to right:
Councillor
Edward Noel
Chorley, Mayor
William Taylor
and Alderman
Vic Steed don
party hats to
raise a laugh
in 1954.
(Sue Jackson)

Wednesbury Carnival Queen is crowned during a luncheon held at the Town Hall, 19 August 1950. Left to right: Mayoress Alderman Ethel Price, Margaret Littley, Patricia June Day, Kathleen Richardson, comedian Harry Rowson. Just visible behind is the Town Hall organ, the gift of Alexander Brogden, first MP for Wednesbury in 1872. It was dismantled in 1953 and removed to St Augustine's Church, Kensington, London. *(Margaret Foster)*

The Market Place was the starting point for the Mesty Croft carnival parade in 1958. The Mayor and Mayoress, Alderman Vic Steed and Henrietta Maude Steed, are joined by the Carnival Princess aboard a horse-drawn landau as a happy crowd gather outside Disturnal's grocers and Riley's Stationers (now Simon's News). *(Sue Jackson)*

Mayor William Arthur Griffiths and the Mayoress are joined by fellow guests during the Annual Charity Ball held at the Town Hall and adjoining Art Gallery in October 1960. Seen to the right of the Mayor are Hannah Waldron and Councillor Leonard Waldron. The Mayor and Mayoress's chains of office were stolen from their display cabinets during a burglary at West Bromwich Town Hall on 7 September 1981. *(Diane Maynard)*

Local politicians at this gathering are, left to right; -?-, Chairman of Darlaston UDC Frank Baker, -?-, Mayor Alderman Vic Steed, Wolverhampton South-West MP John Enoch Powell, -?-. They are pictured in 1958, ten years before Enoch Powell gained notoriety for his so-called 'Rivers of Blood' speech, at Birmingham, on 20 April 1968. Then, he was opposing the Labour Government's proposed Race Relations Bill (aimed at preventing racial discrimination) when his infamous reference was made to 'the River Tiber foaming with much blood'. In the wake of ensuing public unrest, he was sacked from his post as Shadow Defence Minister by Edward Heath, then leader of the Conservative Party. *(Sue Jackson)*

Alderman Vic Steed (fourth left) stands alongside Betty Boothroyd MP (now Baroness Boothroyd) at the House of Commons, *c.* 1974. Miss Boothroyd held the constituency of West Bromwich West, which includes Wednesbury, from 1974 until retiring from politics in October 2000. Born in Dewsbury, West Yorkshire, she held the distinction of becoming the country's first female Speaker of the House of Commons in 1992. *(Sue Jackson)*

7

En Route

Holyhead Road was newly constructed in 1825–6 by the much celebrated engineer Thomas Telford. Its function was to divert the course of the busy London to Holyhead coaching route away from the congested Market Place and narrow High Street. Until recently it was part of the classified A41 primary road which, starting in Marylebone, Greater London, passes through Wednesbury and terminates at Birkenhead, Merseyside. It is the A5 which actually goes to Holyhead Island, North Wales. Here, in 1892, a steam-powered tram approaches the Town Hall and Art Gallery while, in the opposite direction, a cyclist passes the then single-storey post office. In 1996 the A41 classification was transferred to the Black Country New Road and the Holyhead Road was re-numbered the A4196. *(Author's collection)*

Crankhall Lane, now at the centre of the giant Friar Park housing estate, was still a quiet country road when seen here in about 1913. To the left is the boundary wall belonging to Crankhall Farm, where a petrol station forecourt is now situated. The brick cottage opposite stood near today's junction with Keir Road. *(Dr Christopher Cooksey)*

Viewed in 1936 from St Bartholomew's church tower (whose churchyard gates can be seen in the foreground) is Church Street, since re-named Church Hill. This originally fed into the Market Place at Five Ways before being intersected by the new Northern Orbital Bypass in 1969. Top left can be seen a former smithy in Little Hill while bottom right is the rooftop of the Old Library House, a one-time mechanics' institute. Centre right stands St Bartholomew's National School. *(Cyril Beardmore)*

Wood Green Road is pictured by Robert Ryder, printer, of Spring Head, *c.* 1900. The village-like scene is dominated by St Paul's church, built by the Elwell family of nearby Wednesbury Forge and consecrated on 21 August 1874. Far right is The Woodman public house, which was converted into a restaurant in 2003. In between this ornate hostelry and the adjacent cottage was an entry named Woodman Place, where today Woden Road East emerges and crosses the very busy junction of Wood Green Road, to align with Myvod Road on the opposite side. On 31 December 1892 the country's first electric tram operated along this route as part of a newly laid circuit linking Wednesbury with Darlaston, Walsall and Bloxwich. (*Author's collection*)

This rather sylvan view of Wood Green Road, taken in 1897, shows Elwell's Pool, which provided the head of water to turn the millwheels of Wednesbury Forge. Just beyond the horse and cart is the tiny cottage of the sluice operator, where the road crossed the mill stream over the Fleam Bridge. In the trees behind stands Wood Green House, then the home of Alfred Elwell JP. This was demolished in 1957 and replaced with Wood Green High School. St Paul's church can be seen to the right. Today, in brutal contrast, the trees have given way to concrete pillars and tarmac, as Junction 9 of the M6 motorway intersects the now busy Wood Green Road at this very spot! (*Author's collection*)

A deserted Victoria Street, 3 May 1979. This was the shortest route from the Great Western Railway station to the town centre. The bridge in the foreground crosses the London and North Western line to Darlaston. Hickinbottom's 'Electric' Bakery stands in the centre of the picture. The bakery was founded in 1893 and its last loaves were produced in April 1989 before closure. It was demolished in May 1992 and a giant bingo hall complex now stands on the site. *(Mike Horton)*

Bridge Street is so named after the crossing over the River Tame, erected at its southern end by Thomas Telford in 1826. This photograph of 1938 shows its northern extremity where Holyhead Road and Lower High Street meet. The Georgian building, far left, was Lloyds 'Old' Bank, founded by Wednesbury industrialist Sampson Lloyd III (1728–1807). It was replaced with a modern banking hall in 1960. St John's church, Lower High Street, was built in 1846 and demolished in July 1985. At the centre of the road was the White Horse terminus, where Birmingham trams concluded their journey into the Black Country. The last tram ran in Wednesbury on 1 April 1939. To the right of the telephone booth was the London City and Midland Bank. This was demolished on 15 April 1985, and the site now houses Purity Soft Drinks bottling plant. *(National Tramways Museum)*

The dramatic scene above is the aftermath of a motor car accident at the notorious Dartmouth Arms crossroads in Holyhead Road, *c.* 1958. Forty-six accidents were recorded at the traffic light-controlled junction with Dudley Street in the period 1961–4. Its name was derived from the Dartmouth Arms Inn, seen far right, which was demolished in April 1963. Opposite was another well-remembered public house, The Stores, seen to the left of the fire engine. *(C.J.E.J. Selway)*

Onlookers gain a closer view of the stricken motor vehicle. Linda Pickworth's grocery store (right), at 171 Holyhead Road, was one of many buildings demolished to create space for the large traffic island that replaced the junction in the early 1970s. *(C.J.E.J. Selway)*

High Bullen, pictured here in 1959, is that stretch of road between Trouse Lane and Union Street, since made into a dual carriageway. The gardens in the foreground were once the site of the Crown Tubeworks, built by James Russell in 1825. This is now the approach to the swimming baths and leisure centre. Top left was George Croft's steelworks, a remnant of James Russell's empire, demolished in 1989. Next are seen Frederick Horton's corn merchants and the Horse and Jockey Inn, the latter demolished in 1968 with the Tudor buildings following the year later. The billet sheds of the old fire station can be seen below St Bartholomew's church. Further on, a Midland Red bus approaches the Elephant and Castle public house, behind which can be glimpsed the roof of the Hippodrome Theatre in Upper High Street. *(Paul Burkitt)*

The Elephant and Castle was de-licensed in 1960 and by 1962 was converted to G.E. Fynn's motor sales showroom. A decade later the drinks licence was restored, firstly as Rafael's restaurant, then Bannon's nightclub, before further name changes to Tats, Patrick's, J9 and finally Holby's. To the right was the former Borough Cleansing Department, which later housed Sandy Tebbutt's indoor ski slope before demolition in May 1988 for the extension of the neighbouring nightclub. *(Black Country Society)*

This delivery van belonging to S. Hickinbottom & Son, bakers, was repainted with royal insignia to mark the Coronation of Queen Elizabeth II in 1953. The bakery's garage building still survives in Stafford Street, now re-clad and forming the premises of a lorry hire business. (*Black Country Society*)

Bill Webster, the proprietor of Wednesbury Coaches, sits at the wheel of a Bedford Duple motor coach, *c.* 1956. The travel company's garage was located in Portway Road, alongside the Gladstone inn. (*Ann Betteridge*)

Wednesbury's 'Town' railway station was reached down a flight of steps from Stafford Street and was operated by the London and North Western Railway Co. on the South Staffordshire line. It opened on 1 May 1850. Here the platforms are seen from Potter's Lane on 2 June 1961. *(G. Harrop)*

The original wooden booking office of 1850 was replaced with these much more substantial brick-built facilities in September 1863. Here, the southbound platform, with its pedestrian footbridge crossing the line, is seen in about 1966. Just beyond is one of the station's two signal-boxes. The rooftops of houses in Perry Street can be seen far right. The station buildings fell victim to the demolition men in the early 1970s. *(Mike Horton)*

Text on the reverse of this photograph informs us that it was taken on a Sunday afternoon in June 1935 following a terrible thunderstorm, which flooded the track. The gentleman pictured far left is Harry Steventon. *(Gladys Steventon)*

Wednesbury no. 1 signal-box once stood alongside the level crossing at Potters Lane, as seen on 11 October 1981. It has since been dismantled, along with the cast-iron footbridge, and the line is no longer in use. The old police station and St John's church can be seen in the far distance. *(Jack Haddock)*

The River Tame winds its way to the original eighteenth-century Hydes Road bridge, seen in 1911. Mining subsidence and the need to widen the carriageway saw the old structure replaced with a new single-span bridge between the wars. The capstones of the original bridge were re-used atop the abutments of the new crossing. (*Author's collection*)

Further downstream work was carried out on strengthening the riverbanks at the new Crankhall Lane bridge in 1937. The contractor was Tarmac Ltd of Ettingshall, Wolverhampton. The houses alongside have long since been demolished. (*Author's collection*)

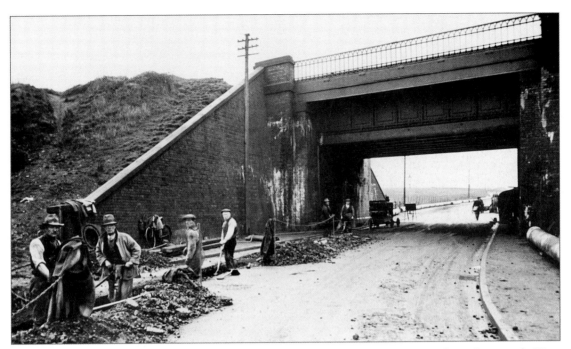

Workmen are seen laying water mains in Hydes Road, Wednesbury, at its boundary with West Bromwich, 18 November 1933. Above them, the Hateley Heath Aqueduct carries the Tame Valley Canal of 1844. The field visible through the opening is where Griffiths and Crockford Roads are now built. *(South Staffs Water plc)*

Canals were once a very important and effective means of conveying haulage across mainland Britain, often incorporating amazing feats of engineering and providing land-locked industrial regions with direct access to the country's chief rivers and ports. One such navigation was the Walsall Canal, cut in 1786–99 and skirting the western approaches to Wednesbury town. Photographed in 1948 at its junction with the Gospel Oak Branch, the industrial scene is intensified by the presence of derelict pit winding gear against the backdrop of the huge Patent Shaft Steelworks. Far left, on the horizon, St Bartholomew's parish church can just be seen. *(Author's collection)*

Above: The German airship Graf Zeppelin looms over Darlaston Road, Kings Hill, on 3 July 1932. Three years earlier it had accomplished the first ever round-the-world flight. The original vessel of 1908 had been designed by Count Ferdinand von Zeppelin (1838–1917). The Atkinson's alehouse, seen far left, was the Barrel Inn, which stood at the corner of Darlington Street. *(Doreen Jones)*

Travelling in a southerly direction, Graf Zeppelin passes over the roofs and chimney pots of Oakeswell Street. Earlier visitations by Zeppelins over Wednesbury skies had been the awful bombings on the night of 31 January 1916 by the airships L19 and L21. Then, at the height of the First World War, fourteen townspeople lost their lives, most coming from the badly hit King Street area. L19 was shot down by Dutch soldiers on its return journey. L21 met the same fate during an assault near Lowestoft, Suffolk, sinking beneath the North Sea on 28 November 1916. *(Jack Cooksey)*

8

Wednesbury Worship

Clothed in neat surplices, the angelic St Bartholomew's parish church boys' choir are joined
by the organist and choirmaster, Gurney Harper (far left) and the Revd Henry William Jones
for this excellent picture, 1944. Back row, left to right: D. Wooding,
A. Blakemore, J. Taylor, D. Westwood, G. Blackhall, G. Rollinson. Middle row: G. Smith,
V. Blyth, G. Webb, K. Moseley, D. Wright, J. Hardisty, W. Birks. Front row: M. Brookes,
A. Trend, M. Vaughan, N. Blakemore, T. Smith, R. Moseley, J. Gilbert, -?-.
(Denys Westwood)

St Bartholomew's parish church in 1897, showing the temporary brick wall that for several years joined the main body of the building with its five-sided apse, which had been relocated further east by Basil Champneys to enlarge the chancel. A permanent connection was made in 1904 with the completion of work to double the size of the south transept. The ringing tower supports a peal of ten bells, the oldest of which is dated 1614. The clock was inserted in 1854. Surrounding the ancient edifice is the windswept burial ground, enlarged by 1 acre in 1823. *(Author's collection)*

Also pictured in 1897 is the church interior showing, to the left of the chancel steps, the finely carved Jacobean pulpit, dated 1611. St Bartholomew's contains fifteen beautiful windows by the great stained glass artist Charles Eamer Kempe MA (1837–1907). *(Author's collection)*

Unique to St Bartholomew's is the fourteenth-century wooden gilded lectern, unusual in its form of a fighting cock, a relic of a once-favoured local blood sport. Studying the rarity in 1957 is Canon Alexander Bannerman Lavelle. The earliest recorded incumbent of the church was one 'Master William' in 1199. (*Wolverhampton Express & Star*)

The last ever recorded entry in the Minutes of the Town Council reads: 'Resolved, that the Mayoral chair in the Council Chamber be given to the Parish Church of St Bartholomew for use as a Bishop's Throne and that a suitably engraved plaque recording the gift by this Council be affixed thereto.' The Revd Peter Gerald Owen is pictured receiving the said gift from the last Mayor, Councillor Arthur Wallace Rawlings, upon the dissolution of the council on 31 March 1966. (*Wolverhampton Express & Star*)

St Mary's Roman Catholic church stands in the aptly named St Mary's Road. It was erected in 1872 to the designs of Sir Gilbert Blount, replacing a church only twenty years old. Originally its steeple was constructed with clay tiles, but they often succumbed to the vicious winds at Wednesbury's highest spot, necessitating their replacement with copper sheeting. To the left is the Presbytery, built in 1852 and now demolished. Just visible far right is the former St Mary's School of 1871, now St Mary's Catholic Social Club. New schools were opened in nearby Manor House Road in 1940. (*Author's collection*)

The highly ornate Our Lady's chapel, *c.* 1900. The panels of the Lady Altar were painted by a Wednesbury inhabitant, Joseph Withers. In the 1890s the church was under serious threat of subsidence from the mine workings of the Hobs Hole colliery beneath. A deal was struck with the mine owners to limit the extent of its operations to 85ft from St Mary's Road. (*Author's collection*)

St John's church stood in Lower High Street from 1846 until its demolition in July 1985. This handsome building was constructed using Peldon stone, which was quarried from Monway Field, beyond Leabrook. In recent years most of the burials have been exhumed, in preparation for a new houseing development that is due to be completed in 2004. (*Author's collection*)

The original St John's Rectory was sited a little further along Lower High Street, its foundation stone having been laid by the Lady of the Manor, Lady Emily Foley, on 22 June 1893. Formerly the Isle of Man Inn had stood on the site. St John's Rectory was later removed to an Edwardian house next door to the library in Hollies Drive. (*Author's collection*)

Pictured at St James's National School in about 1948 are, left to right, John Lewis, the Revd Philip H. Husbands BA, and Bernard Mincher. Mr Husbands (a twin) baptised the author at St James's church in 1962. (*Ann Betteridge*)

The Nativity is performed inside St James's at Christmas 1949. Also constructed with the local Peldon stone, the church was consecrated on 31 May 1848. Perhaps its best-known worshipper was Dorothy Wyndlow Pattison (1832–78), better known as Walsall's celebrated heroine Sister Dora, a personal friend of one-time curate the Revd Richard Twigg. (*Ann Betteridge*)

St James's Parsonage, built in 1849, stood alongside the National School buildings, opposite the church in St James Street. The rambling building decayed rapidly after the vicar took up residence in the former St John's Rectory, Hollies Drive, in the early 1980s. The final blow came after the theft of the roof slates, leading to its demolition in 2000. The school buildings, dating to 1844, still survive as a parish centre. *(Ann Betteridge)*

The Baptist church (centre) was built in 1762, originally to serve Methodist Independents. Today the Holyhead Road building is converted to an ATS motorists' service centre. To the right is the former Anchor Hotel, now used as a dance academy. Far left are Onions general store, the police canteen and 22 Holyhead Road, all of which have now been demolished. This photograph dates from 1968. *(Alan Price)*

This extremely rare picture is of the original Spring Head Methodist chapel, opened on 16 May 1813 and pulled down in 1866 to make way for its successor, this also being demolished when the present Central Mission was opened on 9 March 1968. The first chapel was lit by candles until gas was introduced to the building in 1828. A car park now occupies the site. *(Author's collection)*

Camp Street Primitive Methodist chapel opened on 14 November 1824. Seen here in about 1900, its last meeting was held on 26 June 1966 before eventual demolition in 1970 to provide space for the relocated open market. *(Olive Parker)*

9

Good Companions

Wednesbury Territorials of 'H' Company, 5th Battalion, South Staffs Regiment are seen
at their annual bivouac on land at Glamnachlas Farm, Towyn, on the North Wales coast,
9 August 1909. The 128 non-commissioned officers and men had just completed a
6-mile march on foot to the camp site. It was reported that the average age was twenty
years, the average height 5ft 6in and the average chest measurement 32½in!
Their Wednesbury base was at the Drill Hall, Bridge Street, built in 1893
but now demolished. *(Author's collection)*

Crankhall Farmhouse, Crankhall Lane, is an amazing survivor of Wednesbury's rural origins, sandwiched (as it is today) between a modern doctor's surgery and petrol filling station, the whole being surrounded by the huge Friar Park housing estate. Here, a shooting party poses with the day's game on the farmhouse lawn, *c.* 1915. Standing, left to right, are farmer William Cooksey, Tom Holmes, Mr Wilson, Dr Henry Charles Crew JP and Albert Cooksey. The carriage driver and children are unidentified. *(Dr Christopher J. Cooksey)*

Ploughman Albert Finney turns the soil at Crankhall Farm, aided by two beautiful shire horses. Seen here in about 1910, this field was built over with Walton Road and Warner Road in 1934–5. In the distance are the chimneys of the many tubeworks at nearby Mesty Croft. *(Dr Christopher J. Cooksey)*

During the summer of 1913 Wednesbury's tubeworkers staged a strike, seeking a minimum wage of 23*s* per week, at a time when the industry paid a standard wage of 18*s*. This demonstration was held in Walsall Street outside John Knowles and Sons Tubeworks, founded in 1850. The building was later converted to college buildings, and the site was cleared for a housing development in May 1998. *(Author's collection)*

In 1913 absence from work meant no income! Hungry mouths were fed through the generosity of local merchants supportive of the strikers' plight. Careful examination of the above photograph will reveal that some of these strikers' children are clutching mugs and bowls as they attend a soup kitchen, held in the vicinity of St John's School, Russell Street. *(Brian Broome)*

Hill Top Foundry staff gather at their Smith Road premises in 1940 for an interesting wartime snapshot. The name Wednesbury has been painted out on the signboard (to confuse the enemy in the event of an invasion) while it will be noticed that half the workforce consists of women founders, tackling the jobs vacated by their male counterparts, whose conscription papers had been served. Third left on the third row is the foreman, Edgar Archer. *(Edgar Archer)*

The Ski Room at the Anchor Hotel, Holyhead Road, was a favourite venue for works functions. This is a gathering for Hill Top Foundry's Annual Dinner, *c.* 1955. Presumably invitations didn't include partners! *(Edgar Archer)*

Sewing machinists work a busy shift at the Lower High Street premises of Geoffrey Hughes Ltd, wholesale clothiers, 1954. This was an associate company of Leonard Hughes (Supplies) Ltd, house furnishers of nearby Holyhead Road. The signs reading 'watch your ticket dates' were a reminder to dispatch orders on a first come, first served basis. Second right is Joan Orme, while far right foreground is Margaret Fowler. *(Ann Betteridge)*

Geoffrey Hughes staff celebrate Christmas 1955 at the Anchor Hotel, Holyhead Road. Left to right: Brenda ?, Betty ?, Jean Simmons, -?-, Joan Orme, -?-. *(Jean Simmons)*

Bricklayers take a break from the construction of Riverway, *c.* 1937. A chimney from one of Mesty Croft's tubeworks is to the left of the picture. Third right is Leonard Haffner; far right is Leonard Cox. *(Gladys Cox)*

The small workforce of British Plated Metals at their Smith Road workplace in 1936. Back row, left to right: proprietor Mr Taylor, Alan George, -?-, Gladys Cox, Elsie Jones, Evelyn ?, Tony ?. Front row: Ann Jones, Elsie ?, Mrs Woodcock, Ruby ?, Mr Russell, 'Jonty' Scott. *(Gladys Cox)*

Civil Defence volunteer wardens enter Meeting Street from Trouse Lane during a marching exercise, *c.* 1950. The building with the lamp over a handsome columned doorway was – until 1857 – the Parish Workhouse, established on this site in 1715. Here in 1757 Mary Best, a pauper, was killed by the governess and another. Both were acquitted of the crime. Meeting Street was originally called Workhouse Lane before being re-named after Wednesbury's first Methodist chapel, erected further along the road in 1760 and in use until 1813. *(Katherine Clarke)*

Lorries belonging to Wednesbury Corporation's Public Works Department, were converted to light rescue vehicles for use by the Civil Defence Corps during the Second World War. The name Wednesbury has been painted out on each wagon and their headlamps masked in compliance with wartime regulations. Volunteers such as these supplemented the emergency services in defence of their town, King and country. *(Gladys Cox)*

This gathering of volunteer organisations during the Second World War was opposite the Town Hall in Holyhead Road, at a point where Russell House high-rise flats now stand. The junction of Russell Street with Camphill Lane is far left of the picture. The presence of a brass band indicates that a parade was most likely taking place. (*Sam Stevenson*)

Wartime firewomen practise operating a Beresford Stork water pump, adjacent to the fire station, at Ladbury's Lane, 1940. Firewoman Audrey Clapp faces the camera, leaning on the pump, to the right. (*Jack Cooksey*)

Residents of Terrace Street throw a street party, to celebrate 'Victory in Japan' day, 18 August 1945. Standing at the back, left to right: Rene Thomas, Mrs Bond, ? Bond, Mrs Johnson, Alan Johnson, Marian Bridgwater, -?-, Sally Salt, Laurie Bridgwater, ? Bond. Seated at the table: ? Bond, ? Bond, -?-, ? Fellows, ? Fellows, -?-. *(Laurie Bridgwater)*

Fancy dress was the order of the day for these children celebrating Victory in Europe Day in 1945, possibly at Brunswick Park. Margaret Littley is seen third from right on the second row. *(Margaret Foster)*

Wednesbury volunteer nurses of the British Red Cross Society are pictured at their 'field hospital' tent, *c.* 1959. Left to right: Mrs Goode, Beatrice Craddock, Betty Roberts, Phyllis Berry, Dora Stevenson. *(C.J.E.J. Selway)*

Below: Wednesbury Divisional Special Constabulary gather at the old police station, Holyhead Road, for this formal photograph, Sunday 26 May 1963. Beyond the station yard is St John's church, Lower High Street. Seated front row, fifth from left (with baton), is Wednesbury Police Superintendent I.R. Cogbill. The old police station was demolished on 4 January 1990. *(Tony Mallam)*

Players with Wednesbury Rugby Union Football Club pose for a team photograph at Hydes Road playing fields, *c.* 1955. Today their headquarters at Woden Road North possesses the world's tallest set of rugby goalposts, standing an incredible height of 125ft. *(Christopher Bott)*

This special gathering of veteran cricketers was held at the Wednesbury Sports Union grounds, Wood Green Road, *c.* 1957. Wednesbury Cricket Club was founded in 1875, becoming part of the Sports Union in 1936. Back row, left to right: Umpire ?, Howard Jones, William Townsend, Albert Moreton, William Parkes, Malcolm Whitehouse, Philip Longmore. Front row: Geoffrey Perrins, Leonard Middleton, David Chadwick Jackson, Leonard Dodd, William Weston. *(Geoff Webb)*

The six-piece Avalon Dance Band is pictured on the Town Hall stage in early 1939, just before the outbreak of the Second World War. Left to right: Stan Corfield, Jack Bradney, Tom Harvey, Charles ?, Jack Harrison (aged sixteen), Les Cooper. *(Jack Harrison)*

By the age of twenty-four Jack Harrison was running a very successful band in his own name. Jack (left) shakes hands with MC Bill Jones at a musical evening staged at Wednesbury Conservative Hall, Walsall Street, 1947. *(Jack Harrison)*

The cast of Wednesbury Inner Wheel's Christmas pantomime breaks from costume rehearsal for a publicity picture, *c.* 1960. The thespians are, left to right, Dorothy Smith, Betty Baxter, Madge Brookes, Freda Baker, Ethel Elwell and Rene Naylor. *(Ann Betteridge)*

Pupils of the Marjorie Freeman School of Dance assemble at the rear of a Brunswick Park Road home in uniformed dress, *c.* 1930. The only boy present among fifty-one girls is Jack Benfield. During the Second World War he was taken prisoner before being safely liberated. Marjorie Freeman later married Wednesbury dentist Jack Simcox. Their daughter is the delightful actress Jill Simcox (b. 1935), whose early televison roles were as Sister Arnold in *Emergency Ward Ten* and farmer Linda Ash in *Crossroads.* *(Jack Cooksey)*

The Coronation of Queen Elizabeth II is celebrated in style by the 'Jolly Green Giant' accompanied by three female impersonators at Beech Road, 2 June 1953. Left to right: Jack Mullender, Bill Mullender, John Mullender, Bill Causer. *(Katherine Clarke)*

Children proudly wear their fancy dress costumes for Coronation Day 1953 at Crew Road. Favourite characters were Queen Elizabeth I and circus clowns. The house on whose lawn they are assembled is called Wingate. *(Dorothy Hill)*

These six children celebrating Coronation Day 1953 are pictured in Johnson Road, Friar Park. Left to right: Dennis Blades, Terry Goode, ? Goode, Edna Muckley, -?-, -?-. Nurses' costumes were another popular fancy dress theme of the day. *(Jean Knott)*

Sixth Wednesbury Rover Scouts are pictured in the most unlikely of places – a latrine trench they had just dug! During 1957 a World Jamboree was held to celebrate fifty years of scouting, the main venue being Birmingham's Sutton Park. Sub-camps were located elsewhere in the Midlands, this one being on land owned by the industrialist Colonel Ronald Sankey, near his home Gay Hills at Penn, Wolverhampton, catering mostly for Polish and Belgian scouts. The Wednesbury Rovers acted as wardens. Pictured front to back are Glen Fuller, Terry Burns, -?-, Roger Sutton, Alfred Kirkham, Frank Evans, -?-, John Selway, John Onions, Alan Fuller, Malcolm ?. *(Terry Burns)*

Wednesbury Hippodrome Theatre stood in Upper High Street and originally opened in 1891 as the New Theatre Royal. Seen here are four of the Wednesbury Repertory Company Players from the 1950s. Clockwise from top left: Richard Pescud, Carmen Silvera, John Jarvis, Valerie Gaunt. The actress Carmen Silvera became a household name playing Edith in the television comedy 'Allo, 'Allo, while Valerie Gaunt went on to be a movie victim of that villainous vampire, Dracula. *(Alice Cartwright)*

Sisters Louisa Fellows (left) and Alice Cartwright staff the Hippodrome's immaculate licensed 'artistes' bar, *c.* 1954. Sadly the theatre closed in 1959, the building being demolished and replaced with a supermarket (now Kwik Save) in the early 1960s. *(Alice Cartwright)*

Excited youngsters run alongside the entertainer Hughie Green as he travels along Walsall Street, heading for Brunswick Park, as star guest at the town carnival, 1949. A delivery van from Marsh & Baxter Ltd, Brierley Hill butchers, passes Oakeswell Hall's coachhouse. *(Jack Cooksey)*

Canine contestants and their proud owners await judging of the dog show during the Wednesbury Horticultural Show, *c.* 1950. The show arena was situated within Brunswick Park. Fourth from left is Audrey Clapp with her pet dachshund. *(Jack Cooksey)*

Balloons are released from Brunswick Park during the Horticultural Show, 19 August 1958. The balloon that travelled furthest entitled the finder to a prize on receipt of the attached ticket. The adults, left to right, are -?-, John Stonehouse MP, the Mayor Alderman Vic Steed, Alderman George Wilson Price, -?-, Alderman Ethel Price, the Mayoress Henrietta Maude Steed. *(Sue Jackson)*

Members of Wednesbury Ladies Circle no. 180 celebrate their fifth anniversary by cutting a delicious birthday cake, 30 April 1959. Second right is the Mayoress, Henrietta Maude Steed. *(Sue Jackson)*

Pipe-smoking Mayor Councillor Leonard Waldron assembles with members of the Wednesbury Fellowship of the Disabled as they await the arrival of a coach outside the Town Hall in 1961. Their destination was Weston-super-Mare. *(Diane Maynard)*

Following the 1964 Annual Council Meeting, the ladies retired to a quiet corner of the Art Gallery for drinks. Back row, left to right: Molly Diggett, -?-, -?-, Tina Vernon, Peggy Vernon, Evelyn Stokes, Henrietta Maude Steed, Barbara Ralph, Hannah Waldron, Alderman Ethel Price. Front row: Mrs Morgan and Mrs Berry. *(Jack Stokes)*

Wednesbury MP John Stonehouse and wife Barbara (centre) are pictured surrounded by Labour Party members and their children during a celebration held in the grounds of the Labour Club in Arudel House, Church Hill, in 1958. Serving as Wednesbury's MP for fourteen years, Mr Stonehouse was appointed Parliamentary Secretary to the Ministry of Aviation in November 1964 and was made Postmaster General by 1968. His political career ended in disgrace when – as Walsall North MP – he was jailed for seven years following a much-publicised criminal investigation during 1974 involving the Fraud Squad and his faked disappearance. His actual death was reported on 14 April 1988 when he was aged sixty-two. *(Sue Jackson)*

10

Last Orders

Licensee William S. McGill (second left) is seen sharing a quiet drink with three fellow imbibers outside Ye Olde Leathern Bottel, Vicarage Road, 1909. Reputed to have been built in 1510, the quaint hostelry was enlarged and much altered during renovations carried out in 1913. It is claimed that the notorious highwayman Dick Turpin (1706–39) sampled the ale here. (*Author's collection*)

The red brick and terracotta Talbot Hotel was built on the corner of the Market Place with Spring Head in 1897 for wine merchants John Taylor Duce and Sons, replacing a half-timbered Elizabethan inn. It was pictured in 1906 when owned by Hickman and Pullen's, whose High Bullen brewery supplied its 'Entire' brand of ales. In its time it has been a furnishing store, employment exchange, Co-operative branch, and today it is a post office, undertakers and hairdressers. *(Author's collection)*

The original Horse & Jockey Hotel in Wood Green Road is seen in 1897, just before demolition and the erection of the present building by then licensee Councillor Edwin Butler. The glass palm house was dismantled and re-erected elsewhere. On 14 March 1901 the upstairs billiard room of the new hotel was the scene of the gruesome suicide of William Hartley Edgerton, aged thirty-seven and manager of Edwin Richards Portway Works, who died from a single gunshot wound to the forehead. *(Author's collection)*

This 1897 view of Bridge Street shows two of Wednesbury's oldest public houses standing exactly opposite each other. On the left is the Coachmakers Arms, built in 1726, with its distinctive triple Dutch gables to the frontage. Over the road stood the handsome Red Lion Hotel, a former Georgian coaching inn which was demolished in March 1983. (*Author's collection*)

During the Edwardian period the Coachmakers Arms was given a glazed tile frontage and christened 'The Pretty Bricks' by locals, alluding to the Woodhall's Beefeater panel (left) advertising its West Bromwich brewed ales. Half of its accommodation was demolished to create a link for motorists with Mounts Road. Also, as can be seen in this 1968 picture, the Dutch styling was lost to the front gables, although a little pargetting was added above the upstairs windows. Next door were the offices of Hubert John Barlow's Mounts' Steelworks; he also owned the Wednesbury Hippodrome Theatre. (*Alan Price*)

The Anchor Hotel, Holyhead Road, is captured in 1930 showing its original ornate frontage (see page 97 for modern contrast). Here, every November, the ancient Court Leet was held to transact manorial business. Outside the neighbouring post office stands an early concrete telephone booth. *(Robert Robson)*

Atkinsons' alehouse the Greyhound Inn, 23 Dudley Street, is pictured here in about 1950, ten years before becoming the premises of Brittoll Radiator Services Ltd. It was demolished in the early 1970s. *(Dorothy and Stan Banner)*

The Jolly Collier stood on the corner of Meeting Street and Lloyd Street. It was renamed Collier House when converted to office accommodation but was demolished in March 1991. *(Author's collection)*

A rag and bone man's horse enjoys a feed while its master presumably enjoys a liquid lunch at the Gladstone Inn, Portway Road, 1968. This unspoilt public house still serves today, located only yards from the busy Black Country New Road, though it is no longer frequented by horse-drawn traffic. *(Alan Price)*

Another of Wednesbury's historic old inns was the Nags Head, which stood adjacent to St John's churchyard in Lower High Street, seen here on 3 May 1970. The inn and shops to the right have been replaced with modern residential units. *(Mike Horton)*

Demolition of the Old George Inn, also known as 'Top Wrexham', is captured in this picture, 1959. The replacement pub had already been built further back on the corner site of Upper High Street and Union Street. To the right is Sidney Jowett's poulterers and fruiterers, Walsall Street (now demolished), and the Bell Inn, listed in 1834 as the Blue Bell. This hostelry closed in 1984 but reopened in February 2000 as the Bellwether following extensive restoration and enlargement by Hertfordshire-based architects the Nicholson Partnership. *(C.J.E.J. Selway)*

The Dog and Partridge, Ridding Lane, 8 November 1960. Also visible here is the first dwelling house around the corner in Addison Street. This popular pub was demolished in the late 1980s and replaced with modern housing in 1992. *(Author's collection)*

The Coronation, Friar Park Road, was named after King George VI's monarch-making ceremony, performed on 12 May 1937. Just sixty years later it was demolished to make way for a new discount foodstore. *(Author's collection)*

The Old Park Hotel, pictured on 5 May 1965, stood on Darlaston Road until its demolition in January 1990. It was named after the nearby Old Park Works, operated by the Patent Shaft Company. *(Author's collection)*

Just inside Wednesbury at its boundary with Tipton stood the Boat Inn at Leabrook Road, seen here in 1966. The 'ashes for sale' notice refers to coal cinders which were a cheap surface covering for driveways. Today a massive industrial unit covers the site. *(Author's collection)*

Another Georgian coaching inn built along Thomas Telford's improved Holyhead Road was the Three Swans, which stood opposite the junction with Meeting Street. Seen here in about 1965, it was demolished in 1986 and its site utilised by neighbouring Wednesbury Motors Ltd. On the far right are the residential Monway Buildings. *(Author's collection)*

Standing in Holyhead Road on the corner of St James Street, the Queen's Arms, seen in 1968, was another Georgian hostelry which survives today as a licensed restaurant. To the left, the ladies hair salon is now Ray Buys and Sells and the fish and chip shop is now a Chinese takeaway. Ben Mason potato merchants (right) is today an off-licence. *(Alan Price)*

ACKNOWLEDGEMENTS

The author would like to express his sincere thanks to all the individuals listed below, without whose kindness this book would not have been possible:

Reg Andrews, Edgar Archer, Kate Archer, Dorothy Banner, Stan Banner, Cyril Beardmore, Brian Beasley, Ann Betteridge, Christopher Bott, David Bott, Laurie Bridgwater, Brian Broome, Paul Burkitt, Mary Burkitt, Terry Burns, Mike Campbell, Alice Cartwright, Norma Caswell, Fred Clarke, Katherine Clarke, Sid Clymer, Bridget Coles, Dr Christopher J. Cooksey, Jack Cooksey, Gladys Cox, Bill Day, Katharine Dudley, Bram Dunn, Leslie Flowers, Margaret Foster, Joyce Gill, Kitty Godley, Brenda Greenhough, Jack Haddock, Geoffrey Martin Harper, Paul Harrison, Jack Harrison, G. Harrop, Alan Hill, Joan Hill, Stella Hill, Alan Hollingsworth, Mark Hooper, Mike Horton, Len Hughes, Sue Jackson, Doreen Jones, Jean Knott, Dorothy Lawrence, Margaret Leslie, Kath Lewis, Tony Mallam, Diane Maynard, Sue Mills, Bernard Minton, Joan Paget, Mary Parker, Olive Parker, Christopher Pattison, Norman Pearson, Eric Pell, Alan Price, Terry Price, Doreen Pugh, Freda Riley, Robert Robson, C.J.E. Selway, John Selway, Hilda Shenton, Jill Simcox, Marjorie Simcox, Jean Simmons, Ken Smith, Les Smith, Lilian Smith, Annie Spittle, Pat Stevenson, Sam Stevenson, Gladys Steventon, Evelyn Stokes, Jack Stokes, Malcolm P. Turner, Doreen Underhill, Adrian Waldron, Albert Wassell, Geoffrey Webb, Denys Westwood, Clive Whitehouse, Carol Willetts, Ned Williams.

The author would also like to acknowledge the courtesy of the following organisations:

The *Birmingham Post and Evening Mail*, the Black Country Society, the National Tramway Museum, Old Park Primary School, South Staffs Water plc, the *Wolverhampton Express & Star*.

Smiles all around as this cheerful group raises glasses to toast a successful Annual Council Meeting in 1964. Pictured at the Art Gallery, Holyhead Road, are, left to right, -?-, Councillor James Ralph, Ethel Riley, Alan Hill, Councillor Jack Stokes, Alderman George Wilson Price, -?-. Cheers! *(Jack Stokes)*